D1601069

BOSTON COMMON PRESS
Brookline, Massachusetts

1997

Boston Common Press
17 Station Street
Brookline, Massachusetts 02146

ISBN 0-936184-19-1
Library of Congress Cataloging-in-Publication Data
The Editors of *Cook's Illustrated*

　　　How to make ice cream: An illustrated step-by-step guide to
perfect ice cream, gelato, and sauces/The Editors of *Cook's Illustrated*
1st ed.

　　　Includes 39 recipes and 40 illustrations
　　　ISBN 0-936184-19-1 (hardback): $14.95
　　　I. Cooking. I. Title
1997

Manufactured in the United States of America

Distributed by Boston Common Press, 17 Station Street, Brookline,
MA 02146.

Cover and text design by Amy Klee

HOW TO MAKE ICE CREAM

An illustrated step-by-step guide
to perfect ice cream, gelato, and sauces

THE COOK'S ILLUSTRATED LIBRARY

Illustrations by John Burgoyne

CONTENTS

introduction

OUR FIRST HOUSE IN VERMONT WAS A SMALL cabin in the middle of a pasture bought from old Charlie Bentley, who was known for driving a sea-green Ford down the middle of the road, his eyesight having failed over the years. The whole family pitched in to build the cabin, so the kitchen wasn't much too look at, not more than a simple walk-in arrangement with a small stove, a postage-stamp sink, and walls made of cheap particle board. But I still clearly remember summer evenings, the White Mountain ice cream maker churning away on the floor, the paddle straining as the fresh peach ice cream started to harden. The machine would groan, the motor twisting back and forth in its harness, while the kids added more ice and salt. The first taste was like a naked plunge into a spring-fed river, icy and transforming. The canister was painfully cold, but the wooden paddle was rich with curls and gobs of semifrozen cream flavored with big, ripe peaches trucked in from Pennsylvania. This was the best ice cream in town, and maybe the whole universe.

Although these days I use a fully electric Simac ice cream machine, the Rolls-Royce of the industry, I recently bought a new White Mountain model for the same reason I still use a wind-up watch. It's fun to participate in the process, to turn ice-cream making into a project, not just an end result. There is a more practical reason as well; the old-fashioned freezer holds twice as much as most modern devices, a big benefit in a household with three kids.

This book is about making ice cream with thought and care. We help you purchase a machine, discuss the in-depth testing that went into the master recipe, and then provide you with a range of recipes, from simple chocolate and vanilla, to fruit ice creams, to gelato, to sauces including our favorite hot fudge sauce, which took two months of testing to create.

This book is the fourth in a series of books from *Cook's Illustrated*. The first three titles are *How To Make A Pie*, *How To Make An American Layer Cake*, and *How To Stir-Fry*. New titles in this series are published every two months. For more information about our books, call (800) 611-0759. For information about *Cook's Illustrated* magazine, call (800) 526-8442.

Christopher P. Kimball
Publisher and Editor
Cook's Illustrated

chapter one

ICE CREAM BASICS

THE INGREDIENTS FOR ICE CREAM COULD not be simpler—cream, milk, sugar, flavorings, and sometimes eggs. The results, however, vary greatly, depending on the quantities of each ingredient and the techniques used.

There are two basic types of ice cream. Custard-style ice cream contains egg yolks and has a silky texture and rich flavor. Philadelphia-style ice cream is made without eggs, and often the ingredients are combined without any cooking. It's the difference between a pale yellow French vanilla ice cream and a bright white plain vanilla.

While commercial versions of these two styles abound,

8

we have found that home cooks are better off preparing a custard-type ice cream with egg yolks. These ice creams have the creamy texture we associate with high-quality ice cream. Egg yolks are about 10 percent lecithin, an emulsifier that helps maintain an even dispersal of fat droplets in ice cream and also helps keep ice crystals small. The overall effect is one of richness and smoothness.

Store-bought ice creams made without eggs often contain stabilizers and emulsifiers. Home cooks would not (and generally cannot) add these ingredients to ice cream. Also, commercial ice cream machines are able to inject much more air into Philadelphia-style ice cream than home machines. With more air, these eggless ice creams have a lighter, less icy texture.

Once we decided that custard-style ice creams were the way to go, many other issues arose. How many egg yolks are needed for a one-quart batch of ice cream? What kind of dairy should be used? Cream, half-and-half, milk, or some combination? Also, what's the best way to prepare a custard without causing the eggs to curdle?

We tested as many as eight and as few as three egg yolks in our master recipe. Although five or six eggs deliver an excellent texture, we find the egg flavor becomes too pronounced. Ice cream should taste of dairy, sugar, and flavorings, not like scrambled eggs. Four yolks give ice cream the appropriate silkiness without overpowering other flavors.

The question of which dairy products to use proved more complicated. Ice cream made with all cream is too buttery. The fat content is so high that churning causes tiny particles of butter to form. However, ice cream made with all milk or even half-and-half is too lean. These dairy products contain more water, and the result is an ice cream with tiny ice crystals.

After extensive testing, we came to prefer an equal amount of heavy cream and whole milk. The texture is rich, but there is no butteriness. Most important, there is enough fat to prevent the formation of large ice crystals that might otherwise occur when using a lower-fat dairy combination.

Besides adding sweetness, sugar also promotes a smoother, softer, more "scoopable" end product. This is because sugar reduces the number and size of ice crystals and lowers the freezing temperature of the custard. The latter effect allows you to churn the custard longer before it freezes firm, thus incorporating more air into the ice cream.

In our testing, we found that the texture of a quart of ice cream made with one cup of sugar is excellent, but the sweetness overpowers delicate flavors like vanilla. We tried one-half cup of sugar per quart of ice cream and found that the ice cream was too firm to scoop right from the freezer. The texture was marred by iciness as well. Three-quarters cup sugar is enough to keep the ice cream soft and smooth without making it cloying. Note that bitter flavors like cocoa need to be offset with additional sugar.

With the ingredient issues settled, we turned our focus to questions of technique. We soon discovered that subtle changes in the custard-making process can have a profound effect on texture. Our goal was absolute smoothness and creaminess. Of course, the danger of heating the eggs too high and causing the custard to curdle (the eggs literally clump together, as in making scrambled eggs, and cause the custard to break and become lumpy) also lurks in the background.

Our test kitchen came up with the following list of tips that will guarantee optimum texture and prevent curdling.

■■ PREHEAT MILK AND CREAM WITH SOME SUGAR. We like to heat the milk, cream, and part of the sugar to 175 degrees. Do not heat this mixture any higher, or you may curdle the eggs when you add the mixture to them. Lower temperatures will not dissolve the sugar fully and thus are also not advised.

■■ BEAT YOLKS AND SOME SUGAR. While the milk, cream, and part of the sugar are heating, beat the yolks with the remaining sugar. When making vanilla ice cream, we found that adding unbeaten or lightly beaten yolks to the custard results in an ice cream with a shocking yellow color. Even though color is not an issue in all ice creams (chocolate, for example), we found that prolonged beating—at least two minutes with an electric mixer set to medium-high or four minutes with a whisk—helps dissolve the sugar and evenly disperses the emulsifying agent contained in the yolks. This maximizes the thickening and emulsifying power of the eggs once they are added to the custard.

TEMPER BEATEN YOLKS SLOWLY. Sudden exposure to high heat can curdle eggs and should be avoided. Thus, add a small portion of the hot milk-cream mixture to the beaten eggs in a slow stream, whisking constantly as you pour. Use a towel to hold the bowl containing the yolks in place. This process, called tempering, also thins out the thick yolk-sugar mixture so that it can be more easily incorporated into the hot milk and cream.

HEAT CUSTARD SLOWLY. Whisk the thinned yolks back into the pan with the remaining hot milk and cream. Start heating the custard slowly, and never allow it to boil or it will become lumpy. We found that heating the custard slowly (as opposed to quickly) results in a smoother, thicker texture. Also, you are less likely to curdle a custard set over low heat. Depending on your stove and other variables, plan on at least three minutes, and ideally five to ten minutes, to heat the custard to the proper temperature.

■ TEMPERATURE IS KEY FOR PERFECT CUSTARD. We found that various "tricks" for determining when a custard is fully cooked are only minimally helpful. Yes, a custard does thicken enough to coat the back of a spoon. Yes, a custard should hold its shape when a line is drawn through it on the back of the spoon. But these things may happen well before the custard has reached 180 degrees, the temperature we find ideal for ice cream making. Since egg yolks start to curdle between 185 and 190 degrees, our recommended final temperature of 180 degrees provides some margin of error but allows the eggs to provide a maximum amount of thickening. A custard cooked to only 160 or 170 degrees will make a slightly less rich, less silky ice cream. For this reason, we advocate the use of an instant-read thermometer when making custard for ice cream.

■ STRAIN CUSTARD FOR BETTER TEXTURE. No matter how careful you are, tiny bits of egg may overcook and form thin particles or strands, especially around the edges and bottom of the pan. Pouring the cooked custard through a fine-mesh strainer will eliminate any of these solid egg pieces. However, a curdled custard with large clumps of eggs cannot be rescued and should be discarded.

■■ CHILL, CHILL, CHILL. It's imperative that you chill the custard fully before placing it in an ice cream machine. We found that chilling the custard to 40 degrees or lower is ideal. We also found that if the custard is too warm when it is placed in the ice cream machine, it will need to be churned for much longer (up to an hour) until frozen to a semisolid state. Ice cream machines with canisters that require freezing before churning will loose their cooling ability before this stage is reached. Ice cream machines with self-contained freezers can bring warm custards down to the correct temperature, but the extra churning causes the formation of butter flecks.

■■ DO NOT CHURN TOO LONG. Ice cream will not emerge from any ice cream maker (including those that cost $500) with a firm texture. Once the ice cream is well chilled (about 25 degrees), fluffy, and frozen to the texture of soft-serve ice cream, remove it from the ice cream maker. It takes about thirty minutes of churning to reach this stage in most ice cream machines. If you churn any longer, you may promote the development of butter flecks. In any case, further churning will not freeze ice cream any harder. Several hours in the freezer will complete the freezing process.

WAIT FOR ADD-INS. Nuts, chocolate, raisins, cookies, and other small items should be added to ice cream just before the churning is completed. We generally add them right to the ice cream maker and allow it to churn for another thirty seconds to distribute them. If you allow the ice cream maker to churn any longer, the blade will start to smash and eventually pulverize your add-in ingredients.

STORE IN AIRTIGHT CONTAINER. Once the ice cream has been churned to the consistency of soft ice cream, turn off the ice cream machine and transfer the ice cream to a nonreactive container. We like plastic containers with airtight lids. Ideally, we prefer to put the ice cream in the freezer for two to four hours before serving. It will emerge soft and silky. Homemade ice cream can be frozen for up to two days. If kept longer, homemade ice cream becomes icy and loses much of its flavor.

WARM BEFORE SERVING. If you store ice cream for more than a few hours, the texture will become firm, like that of the ice cream sold in supermarket freezer cases. If you prefer a softer texture, transfer the container with the ice cream to the refrigerator thirty minutes to one hour before serving. We find that ice cream tastes best around 10 to 12 degrees.

chapter two

EQUIPMENT

A N ICE CREAM MACHINE IS, OF COURSE, essential for making the recipes in this book. A few other kitchen tools will help ensure perfect results.

ICE CREAM MACHINE

There are four general types of ice cream machines, each with pros and cons for the home cook. Your choice will be affected by your budget and how frequently you prepare ice cream.

All ice cream machines are able to sustain temperatures below 32 degrees; however, each type does this differently. Subfreezing temperatures are needed because sugar lowers the freezing temperature of ice cream to around 27 or 28 degrees. More sugar or the presence of alcohol lowers the freezing temperature even more.

Old-fashioned ice cream makers, which rely on ice and rock salt and come with either a manual or electric churning mechanism, were the standard until the late 1970s (*see* figure 1, page 24). The chilled custard is placed in a central container that is surrounded by ice and salt. Like sugar, salt lowers the freezing temperature of liquids. By adding a lot of rock salt (which melts more slowly than table salt), the temperature of the brine falls well below 32 degrees. This in turn lowers the temperature of the custard and allows it to freeze into ice cream as it is churned.

We find that these traditional models in wooden buckets are messy to use. They are also less reliable than more modern ice cream machines because they can be affected by ambient conditions. Hot weather makes it more difficult to keep the brine below 32 degrees, so the ratio of salt to ice may need to be altered. In general, we find that using these ice cream makers requires practice and patience and that the results are not guaranteed.

However, many of these bucket-type machines have a two-quart capacity, double that of all other ice cream machines designed for home use. Also, there are no parts to prefreeze, so this type of ice cream maker may be appropriate if your freezer is very crowded or runs well above 0 degrees. You may also make successive batches in this type of ice cream maker.

Expect to spend $100 for a traditional bucket-style ice cream machine with hand crank. Models with electric churning mechanisms generally cost about $150. These machines are increasingly hard to find. Old-fashioned hardware stores are the best bet.

Ice cream making at home changed with the invention of the Donvier in the late 1970s (*see* figure 2, page 25). Its French-sounding pedigree notwithstanding, the name actually comes from the Japanese for "very cold." This ingenious invention was created by a Japanese engineer who thought of the idea after one of his children accidentally spilled milk on an aluminum cooling tray for sushi. He redesigned the tray, which housed a powerful coolant, into a canister shape more appropriate for ice cream making.

To use this type of ice cream machine, you must first place the aluminum canister filled with the patented super-coolant in the freezer overnight. The metal canister is about one inch thick and is hollow. The coolant, which is akin to antifreeze, is contained inside the hollow walls of the canister and is capable of reaching very low temperatures.

To make ice cream, a chilled custard is poured into the very cold canister, which fits into a plastic shell, and a plastic hand crank is attached for churning. The home cook must turn the crank every few minutes to scrape away the portion of the custard that has frozen onto the inside of the canister. The crank should not be turned too often, or the custard will not get a chance to freeze. Eventually, all of the unfrozen custard rests against the supercold metal and freezes.

Although inexpensive (about $50), these ice cream machines do have some drawbacks. They do not freeze ice cream as solid as some other machines do. You will definitely need to transfer ice cream to the freezer for several hours before serving. In addition, these machines require space in a very cold freezer to work. If your freezer is very crowded and/or too warm (temperatures significantly above 0 degrees will not work), the coolant will not get cold enough and the ice cream will not freeze properly. Last, because so little churning is involved, these machines do not beat much air into ice cream. The texture is not as smooth or fluffy as ice cream made in more expensive machines.

One last drawback is that this machine can only make one quart of ice cream a day. To make a second batch, the canister must be frozen for at least twelve hours before the next use. If you buy or own this type of ice cream maker, we suggest that you leave it in the freezer at all times so that you can make ice cream without advance planning.

A relatively new variation on this type of ice cream

machine adds an electric churning mechanism (*see* figure 3, page 26). An electric motor rests on top of the lid and powers the churning blade. The benefits are obvious. Constant churning beats in more air and results in a smoother texture and less iciness. These models generally cost around $75 (sometimes less) and are a good value. We prefer them to the standard Donvier. We have had good success with the Krups La Glacière in our test kitchen. An additional canister can be purchased with this model so that two batches of ice cream can be prepared on the same day.

Without a doubt, ice cream machines with self-contained electric freezers are the best choice for home use. Modeled on commercial machines, these units are twice the size of a standard food processor and weigh thirty pounds or more. The custard is poured into a metal bowl that sits in the large countertop unit, which also houses a small freezer. Two switches activate the freezer and a powerful churning blade.

We love our Simac machine from Italy (*see* figure 4, page 27), but the $500 price tag will be an impediment to all but the most dedicated ice cream maker. This Rolls-Royce of ice cream makers turns out frozen desserts with ultimate smoothness and no iciness. There is no down time between batches, and ice cream emerges at a significantly lower temperature and hence with a firmer texture than from other ice cream machines. Ice cream can be served right from this machine without further hardening in the freezer.

▟ INSTANT-READ THERMOMETER

The precise measurement of temperature is essential in the preparation of ice cream. Custards should be cooked to 180 degrees for optimum thickening, but no higher because curdling becomes a danger. Likewise, custards should be fully cooled below 40 degrees to promote quick churning and freezing without the formation of butter flecks.

For these reasons, we recommend the use of an instant-read thermometer when making ice cream. Since it is also helpful to measure the temperature of ice cream at serving time (we find ice cream tastes best around 10 to 12 degrees), choose an instant-read thermometer that goes down to 0 degrees.

You may also want to check the temperature of your freezer, especially if using an ice cream machine with a canister that must be frozen overnight. A freezer/refrigerator thermometer that registers temperatures below zero can be purchased for several dollars at any housewares store. Cold freezer temperatures (below zero) are required for optimum performance of frozen canister-type ice cream machines. Note that removing frost and excess food can lower the freezer temperature by several degrees. However, if your freezer continues to run well above zero (say, 5 degrees or higher), you will be better off using an ice cream machine that does not require prefreezing of any parts.

▐▐ SAUCEPAN

Custards are best cooked over low heat in a tall, heavy saucepan that will prevent scorching. A two-and-one-half-quart saucepan is ideal. You may want to consider a pan with a nonstick surface. It certainly will be easier to clean.

Whether you choose a conventional or nonstick surface, look for a sturdy but not overly heavy saucepan that weighs between two and three pounds. Pans that weigh four or five pounds will be difficult to lift when filled. Lighter pans that weigh less than two pounds will be prone to scorching.

We prefer pans with heatproof handles. It's much easier to stir the custard constantly if you can hold the handle without a dish towel or pot holder. We have had good experiences with All-Clad saucepans in our test kitchen and recommend them highly.

▐▐ STRAINER

A fine-mesh strainer picks out tiny bits of egg that sometimes form in well-made custards. These bits of egg would otherwise mar the texture of the ice cream, so they must be removed. Fine-mesh strainers can also be used to strain out ground nuts from steeped liquids or to remove seeds from berries. We particularly like a conical-shaped French sieve called a chinois. The very fine mesh traps even the smallest particles. The shape makes it easy to press down on solids, like nuts and berries, to extract as much liquid, and therefore flavor, from them as possible.

Figure 1.

Traditional ice cream makers in wooden buckets can be less reliable than more modern ice cream machines because they can be affected by ambient conditions. Also, you will need to track down rock salt at a hardware store. However, many models have a large capacity, and this type of ice cream maker does not require prefreezing of any parts. As long as you have a steady supply of ice and rock salt, successive batches of ice cream may be made in this kind of machine. We prefer models, like this one, with electric churning mechanisms.

Figure 2.
The Donvier revolutionized ice cream making at home.
A supercoolant inside the central metal canister lowers the tem-
perature of the custard as you churn with the plastic hand crank.
This model is a good choice if your freezer maintains a tempera-
ture at or below zero. Note that the metal canister must be
refrozen overnight before making a second batch of ice cream.

Figure 3.
Similar to the Donvier, this Krups ice cream machine has an
electric motor in the base that rotates the metal canister while a
stationary blade churns. The constant motion beats more air into
the ice cream and results in a better texture. For this reason, we
prefer an electric churning mechanism.

Figure 4.
The Rolls-Royce of ice cream machines, this Simac unit contains
its own freezer. The texture of ice cream made in this machine is
superb, and the ice cream may be eaten right after churning without further hardening in the freezer. This machine can be used to
make successive batches of ice cream on the same day. If money is
no object, this kind of ice cream machine is the best choice.

chapter three

ᕶ

CLASSIC
ICE CREAMS

THIS CHAPTER CONTAINS RECIPES FOR ALL the classics—vanilla, chocolate, coffee— as well as nut ice creams and those flavored with exotic ingredients like ginger and coconut. Ice creams made with fresh fruits require special techniques because of the moisture content in the fruit. These ice creams are covered in the following chapter. This chapter focuses on ice creams made with "dry" flavorings that do not upset the proportions in the custard.

Vanilla ice cream is the basis for all the ice cream and

gelato recipes in this book. While the use of a vanilla bean makes a tremendous difference in this recipe, we have found that vanilla extract makes more sense for other flavors. The extract complements the flavors of chocolate, coffee, and nuts, while vanilla beans tend to overwhelm them.

When using a vanilla bean, pistachio nuts, or dried coconut, it is necessary to add an extra step to the basic custard-making process. These ingredients are steeped in almost-simmering milk and cream for about thirty minutes. They give up their flavor to the dairy ingredients, which are then used to temper the beaten egg yolks.

Other nuts, such as walnuts for Maple Walnut Ice Cream or pecans for Butter Pecan Ice Cream, are simply added at the end of the churning process. In these recipes, the nuts provide textural and flavor contrasts to the base. However, they are not used to flavor the custard itself.

Chocolate, coffee, and ginger flavors are best added in dry form, such as cocoa powder, instant espresso powder, or ground ginger. Using the liquid forms of these flavorings (like brewed coffee or a sugar syrup made with fresh ginger) adds extra water to the custard and can cause iciness. Melted chocolate can be used in small amounts to enrich a basic chocolate ice cream. However, we found that the fat in melted chocolate can be quite heavy on the tongue if used in large amounts or as the sole provider of chocolate.

Master Recipe

Vanilla Ice Cream

NOTE: Two teaspoons of vanilla extract may be substituted for the vanilla bean, although the flavor will not be as true. To maximize the extract's potency, stir it into the chilled custard just before churning. Figures 5–12, pages 33–38, illustrate the custard-making process. This recipe yields about one quart, as do all the ice cream and gelato recipes in this book.

1½	cups whole milk
1½	cups heavy cream
¾	cup sugar
1	4-inch piece of vanilla bean, slit lengthwise and seeds removed (*see* figures 13 and 14, page 39)
4	large egg yolks

Master Instructions

1. Combine milk, cream, ½ cup sugar, and vanilla seeds and pod in heavy 2½-quart saucepan set over medium heat. Bring mixture to 175 degrees, stirring occasionally to dissolve sugar and break up vanilla seeds.

2. Meanwhile, beat remaining ¼ cup sugar and yolks in medium bowl, scraping down sides as needed, until mixture turns pale yellow and thickens so that it falls in ribbons, about 2 minutes with electric mixer on medium-high or 4 minutes with whisk.

3. Remove about ½ cup hot milk-cream mixture from pan and slowly whisk into beaten yolk mixture. Gradually whisk thinned yolk mixture back into saucepan. Reduce heat to low and bring mixture to 180 degrees, stirring constantly, about 5 minutes. Custard should be thick but not curdled or boiled.

4. Remove saucepan from heat; pour custard through fine-mesh strainer and into nonreactive bowl or container. Retrieve vanilla pod from strainer and add to custard. Place bowl in larger *(continued on next page)*

Master Instructions
Vanilla Ice Cream

4. *(continued from previous page)* bowl of ice water to bring custard to room temperature.

5. Cover bowl and refrigerate until custard registers 40 degrees or lower on thermometer, 4 to 8 hours. (Custard may be refrigerated overnight.) Remove vanilla pod from custard (or add extract, if using), stir well, and then pour custard into ice cream machine. Churn until frozen but still a bit soft. (Do not over-process or ice cream may become icy with flecks of butter.) Transfer ice cream to nonreactive container, seal, and freeze until firm. (Ice cream will keep up to 2 days.)

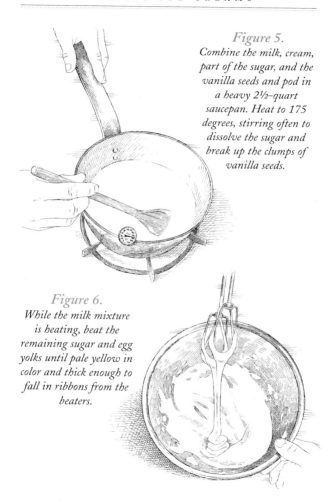

Figure 5.
Combine the milk, cream,
part of the sugar, and the
vanilla seeds and pod in
a heavy 2½–quart
saucepan. Heat to 175
degrees, stirring often to
dissolve the sugar and
break up the clumps of
vanilla seeds.

Figure 6.
While the milk mixture
is heating, beat the
remaining sugar and egg
yolks until pale yellow in
color and thick enough to
fall in ribbons from the
beaters.

Figure 7.
Use a dish towel to steady the bowl containing the beaten yolks.
Slowly whisk about ½ cup of the hot milk mixture into the yolks
to thin them out. Then whisk the thinned yolks into the
saucepan.

Figure 8.
Stirring constantly, heat the custard over low until thick and a
temperature of 180 degrees has been reached. The custard should
be thick enough so that a line drawn through it on the back of a
spoon holds for several seconds. For a more precise measurement,
use an instant-read thermometer.

Figure 9.
Pour the custard through a fine-mesh strainer to remove any curdled bits and into a nonreactive bowl. Add the vanilla pod back
to the custard.

Figure 10.
Chill the custard to room temperature in a bowl of ice water.
Cover the bowl and refrigerate until the custard reaches a tem-
perature below 40 degrees.

36

Figure 11.
Remove and discard the vanilla pod. (If using vanilla extract
instead of a vanilla bean, add it now.) Pour the custard into an
ice cream machine and churn.

Figure 12.
Depending on the ice cream machine, it will be necessary to
churn the custard for about 30 minutes. At this point, the volume
should be increased by about 25 percent, and the ice cream will be
soft and fluffy. Scoop the ice cream into a nonreactive container
and freeze it until firm before serving.

Figure 13.
A vanilla bean adds the truest flavor to vanilla ice cream.
To flavor the custard, cut a 4-inch piece of vanilla bean in half
lengthwise with a small, sharp knife.

Figure 14.
Place the knife at one end of the vanilla bean half and press
down to flatten the bean as you move the knife away from you
and remove the seeds. Add the seeds and pod to the saucepan
with the milk and cream.

3 9

Chocolate Chip Ice Cream

➤ **NOTE:** *This simple variation adds small chunks of a high-quality chocolate bar to vanilla ice cream made with extract in place of the vanilla bean. See figure 15 for information on chopping a chocolate bar for ice cream.*

1½	**cups whole milk**
1½	**cups heavy cream**
¾	**cup sugar**
4	**large egg yolks**
1	**teaspoon vanilla extract**
2	**ounces bittersweet or semisweet chocolate bar, chopped**

INSTRUCTIONS:

Follow Master Recipe instructions for Vanilla Ice Cream (*see* page 30), adding chocolate about 30 seconds before churning is completed.

VARIATIONS:

For Mint Chocolate Chip Ice Cream, replace vanilla extract with ¼ cup clear or green crème de menthe.

For Oreo Ice Cream, replace chocolate with 1 cup coarsely crumbled Oreo cookies (*see* figure 16) about 30 seconds before churning is completed.

40

Figure 15.

Bittersweet or semisweet chocolate bars make an excellent addition to ice cream because they are already quite thin. Blocks of chocolate are harder to use because they yield irregular chunks that are often quite thick. Chop a thin chocolate bar into ¼-inch pieces.

Figure 16.

Any favorite cookies, including Oreos, gingersnaps, almond biscotti, or even brownies, may be added to ice cream. To crumble cookies, place them in a zipper-lock plastic bag and crush them with your fist or the bottom of a glass. Do not crush the cookies into fine crumbs.

41

Chocolate Ice Cream

➤ **NOTE:** *Cocoa powder gives ice cream a strong chocolate flavor without adding any more richness or fat. Dutch-process cocoa has a smoother flavor than that of natural cocoa and is preferred in this recipe. Two more tablespoons of sugar are needed to offset the bitterness of unsweetened cocoa. Note that cocoa powder makes the egg yolk mixture very thick, so whisk in the hot milk quite slowly to incorporate it evenly. The cocoa also increases the amount of time needed to thicken the custard by several minutes.*

1½	cups whole milk
1½	cups heavy cream
⅞	cup sugar
4	large egg yolks
⅓	cup unsweetened cocoa powder, preferably Dutch-process
1	teaspoon vanilla extract

■ INSTRUCTIONS:

Follow Master Recipe instructions for Vanilla Ice Cream (*see* page 30), increasing sugar in step 1 to ⅝ cup. Stir cocoa into thickened egg yolk–sugar mixture with rubber spatula (*see* figure 17); beat until fully incorporated.

🌿

Figure 17.
Use a rubber spatula to stir the cocoa powder into the thickened
egg yolk–sugar mixture. Once the cocoa has been moistened, use
an electric mixer or a whisk to incorporate the cocoa fully.

43

Chocolate Truffle Ice Cream

➤ NOTE: *The addition of melted bittersweet chocolate gives this ice cream an especially rich chocolate flavor. It also makes the beaten egg yolk mixture very thick and stiff. Slowly add the hot milk to thin out the egg yolk mixture gradually.*

1½	cups whole milk
1½	cups heavy cream
¾	cup sugar
4	large egg yolks
⅓	cup unsweetened cocoa powder, preferably Dutch-process
4	ounces bittersweet chocolate, melted and cooled
1	teaspoon vanilla extract

■ INSTRUCTIONS:

Follow Master Recipe instructions for Vanilla Ice Cream (*see* page 30), stirring cocoa into thickened egg yolk–sugar mixture with rubber spatula (see figure 17, page 43). Stir in melted chocolate and beat with electric mixer until fully incorporated.

▋ VARIATIONS:

Follow recipe for either Chocolate Ice Cream (*see* page 42) or Chocolate Truffle Ice Cream to make these variations.

For Chocolate Chocolate Chip Ice Cream, add 2 ounces chopped bittersweet or semisweet chocolate bar about 30 seconds before churning is completed. See figure 15, page 41, for information on chopping a chocolate bar for ice cream.

For Chocolate Oreo Ice Cream, fold in 1 cup coarsely crumbled Oreo cookies about 30 seconds before churning is completed. See figure 16, page 41, for information on crumbling cookies for ice cream.

For Rocky Road Ice Cream, fold in ½ cup slivered blanched almonds and 1 cup mini marshmallows about 30 seconds before churning is completed.

Coffee Ice Cream

➤ **N O T E :** *Instant espresso powder dissolves completely in the custard and does not leave any gritty residue like coffee grounds.*

1½	cups whole milk
1½	cups heavy cream
¾	cup sugar
3	tablespoons instant espresso powder
4	large egg yolks
1	teaspoon vanilla extract

■■ I N S T R U C T I O N S :

Follow Master Recipe instructions for Vanilla Ice Cream (*see* page 30), stirring espresso powder into milk-cream mixture in step 1.

■■ V A R I A T I O N S :

For Mocha Chip Ice Cream, add 2 ounces chopped bittersweet or semisweet chocolate bar about 30 seconds before churning is completed. See figure 15, page 41, for information on chopping a chocolate bar for ice cream.

For Coffee Oreo Ice Cream, fold in 1 cup coarsely crumbled Oreo cookies about 30 seconds before churning is completed. See figure 16, page 41, for information on crumbling cookies for ice cream.

Caramel Almond Swirl Ice Cream

➤ **N O T E :** *Caramel can be tricky to prepare. Begin by heating the sugar in a deep saucepan without stirring. At the very first wisp of smoke, start stirring until all the sugar is dissolved. Cook the sugar until it is light honey in color, which should take ten minutes or less. If the sugar becomes any darker, the caramel will be too stiff to swirl into the ice cream. Toasted and chopped walnuts, pecans, or macadamia nuts may be substituted for the almonds if desired. See figure 18, page 48, for information on toasting nuts in a dry skillet.*

1½	cups whole milk
1½	cups heavy cream
¾	cup sugar
4	large egg yolks
1	teaspoon vanilla extract

Caramel Almond Swirl

½	cup sugar
⅜	cup heavy cream
½	cup chopped almonds, toasted

∷ I N S T R U C T I O N S :

Follow Master Recipe instructions for Vanilla Ice Cream (*see* page 30). While custard is chilling, prepare Caramel Almond Swirl. Heat sugar in deep saucepan set over low heat without stirring. At first wisp of smoke, stir constantly with long-handled spoon until *(continued on next page) (continued from previous page)* sugar melts and caramel is light golden color, 8 to 10 minutes. Carefully add cream, making sure to keep hands and face away from bubbling sauce. Stir to incorporate cream and cook until sauce has softened again and is smooth, about 2 minutes. Remove pan from heat and pour sauce into glass measuring cup. Stir in almonds and set aside. About 1 minute before churning is completed, place measuring cup in bowl of hot water to heat caramel sauce. Drizzle sauce over frozen ice cream, folding very gently to keep swirl distinct (*see* figure 19).

Figure 18.
To maximize their flavor, place the chopped nuts in a dry skillet set over medium heat and toast, shaking the pan occasionally to turn the nuts, until fragrant, about 5 minutes.

Figure 19.
To keep the caramel swirl distinct, pour the sauce over the frozen
ice cream and then very gently fold to distribute the sauce evenly
throughout the ice cream.

49

Pistachio Ice Cream

➤ **NOTE:** *Unlike artificially flavored and colored bright green versions, this pistachio ice cream tastes like nuts. The color is tan and comes from shelled, unsalted nuts sold in health foods stores. The nuts are toasted to bring out their flavor, ground, infused into the milk, and then strained out. If you want, fold in an additional one-third cup toasted, chopped nuts when the churning is almost completed.*

¾	cups whole milk
1¾	cups heavy cream
1¼	cups shelled, unsalted pistachio nuts, toasted (*see* figure 18, page 48) and ground fine in food processor
¾	cup sugar
4	large egg yolks
½	teaspoon vanilla extract

⠿ INSTRUCTIONS:

Follow Master Recipe instructions for Vanilla Ice Cream (*see* page 30), heating milk and cream almost to boiling point. Add nuts to hot milk and cream and steep 30 minutes. Pour milk-cream mixture through fine-mesh strainer and into clean saucepan, pressing down on nuts to extract as much liquid as possible (*see* figure 20). Discard nuts. Proceed with recipe step 1, heating flavored milk and cream and ½ cup sugar to 175 degrees.

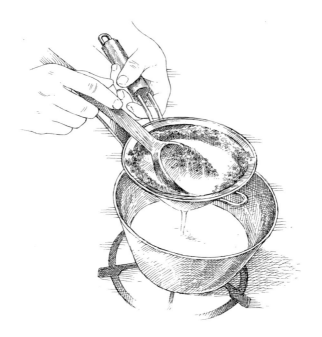

Figure 20.
Finely ground nuts are steeped in almost-simmering milk and cream for 30 minutes to release their flavor. Pour the nuts and milk-cream mixture through a fine-mesh strainer and then use the back of a large spoon or wooden spatula to press on the nuts to extract every bit of liquid and flavor from them. Discard the nuts and then use the flavored milk-cream mixture to make a custard.

Maple Walnut Ice Cream

➤ NOTE: *Maple syrup takes the place of the sugar in the Master Recipe. Pecans may be substituted for the walnuts if desired.*

1	cup plus 2 tablespoons whole milk
1	cup plus 2 tablespoons heavy cream
¾	cup maple syrup
3	large egg yolks
1	teaspoon vanilla extract
¾	cup chopped walnuts, toasted (*see* figure 18, page 48)

∷ INSTRUCTIONS:

Follow Master Recipe instructions for Vanilla Ice Cream (*see* page 30), omitting sugar and heating all of syrup with milk and cream. Beat egg yolks until smooth and lightened in color; thin with hot milk-cream-syrup mixture. About 30 seconds before churning is completed, add nuts.

Butter Pecan Ice Cream

➤ **NOTE:** *Light brown sugar gives this ice cream its character-istic caramel flavor. Because of the additional fat provided by the butter, the ratio of milk to cream has been changed in this recipe.*

2   cups whole milk
1   cup heavy cream
½   cup firmly packed light brown sugar
2   tablespoons unsalted butter
¼   cup granulated sugar
4   large egg yolks
1   teaspoon vanilla extract
¾   cup chopped pecans, toasted
     (*see* figure 18, page 48)

∷ INSTRUCTIONS:

Follow Master Recipe instructions for Vanilla Ice Cream (*see* page 30), replacing ½ cup sugar in step 1 with equal amount of light brown sugar and adding butter to milk-cream mixture. Beat granulated sugar with yolks as directed in Master Recipe. About 30 seconds before churning is completed, add nuts.

Ginger Ice Cream

➤ **NOTE:** *Ground ginger adds a potent punch to this Asian-inspired ice cream. If desired, fold in one-quarter cup minced crystallized ginger just before the churning is completed.*

1½	**cups whole milk**
1½	**cups heavy cream**
2	**teaspoons ground ginger**
¾	**cup sugar**
4	**large egg yolks**
½	**teaspoon vanilla extract**

INSTRUCTIONS:

Follow Master Recipe instructions for Vanilla Ice Cream (*see* page 30), stirring ginger into ½ cup sugar (*see* figure 21) and then adding mixture to milk and cream in step 1.

Figure 21.
Ground spices like ginger and cinnamon can give ice cream a
rich, warm flavor. To prevent ground spices from clumping up,
stir the spice and sugar together in a small bowl and then heat
this mixture along with the milk and cream until dissolved.

Toasted Coconut Ice Cream

➤ **NOTE:** *This ice cream has a strong tropical flavor. Grated unsweetened coconut delivers the best flavor. Look for this product in health foods stores. Sweetened flaked coconut is much less flavorful and should not be used in this recipe. Toasting the coconut brings out its flavor.*

1¾	**cups whole milk**
1¾	**cups heavy cream**
2	**cups unsweetened grated coconut, toasted (*see* figure 22)**
¾	**cup sugar**
4	**large egg yolks**
½	**teaspoon vanilla extract**

⁝ INSTRUCTIONS:

Follow Master Recipe instructions for Vanilla Ice Cream (*see* page 30), heating milk and cream almost to boiling point. Add coconut to hot milk and cream and steep 30 minutes. Pour milk-cream mixture through fine-mesh strainer and into clean saucepan, pressing down on coconut to extract as much liquid as possible (*see* figure 20). Discard coconut. Proceed with recipe step 1, heating flavored milk and cream and ½ cup sugar to 175 degrees.

Figure 22.

To toast unsweetened grated coconut, divide it between
two pie pans. Place the pans in a 300-degree oven and
bake, turning the coconut several times, until golden,
about 15 minutes. Do not let the coconut burn, or it will
impart a bitter flavor to the custard.

chapter four

FRUIT ICE
CREAMS

S
UMMER IS THE BEST TIME FOR MAKING ICE
cream, and with so many fruits in season, the
combination is a natural. However, using fresh
fruits to flavor ice cream presents challenges for
the home cook.

Most fruits contain a high percentage of water, which
can make ice creams icy. We found that fruit ice creams will
never be as silky or creamy as ice creams flavored with vanilla beans or instant espresso powder. The addition of the
fruit itself as well as the additional liquid are antithetical to
creaminess.

While we would never argue for the use of artificial fruit

flavors (the solution employed by many commercial ice cream manufacturers), we do think some extra steps are necessary when working with fresh fruits.

For instance, we like to strain out the seeds and fibers in raspberries, blackberries, and bananas because they can detract from the texture of ice cream. Pushing these fruits through a fine-mesh strainer results in a smooth puree that captures their flavors but does not contain annoying seeds or strings.

Other fruits, such as peaches and cherries, are so juicy (i.e., watery) that we find it best to sauté them with a little sugar to drive off some of their moisture. This process also caramelizes some of the natural sugars in the fruit and makes the fruit flavor more intense. We find that adding these fruit mixtures at the end of churning maximizes creaminess and keeps the fruit flavors fresh and intense.

Despite the additional sweetness provided by the fruit, we discovered that keeping the sugar at the same level as in the Master Recipe (three-quarters cup per quart of ice cream) helps promote smoothness and also intensifies the fruit flavors. In some recipes, we have increased the sugar slightly to offset tartness in the fruit (as with raspberries and blackberries) or excessive moisture (as with cherries).

The ice cream recipes that follow capture the essence of each fruit while maintaining as much creaminess and silki-ness as possible.

Strawberry Ice Cream

➤ **N O T E :** *Really ripe fruit that is red right through to the center is essential in this recipe. The fruit is sprinkled with sugar and allowed to soften in the refrigerator. The chunky fruit puree is added to the ice cream just before the churning is completed.*

1	cup plus 2 tablespoons whole milk
1	cup plus 2 tablespoons heavy cream
¾	cup sugar
3	large egg yolks
1½	cups strawberries (about 6 ounces), hulled and sliced
1	teaspoon vanilla extract

I N S T R U C T I O N S :

Follow Master Recipe instructions for Vanilla Ice Cream (*see* page 30), adding 5 tablespoons sugar to milk-cream mixture in step 1 and ¼ cup sugar to egg yolks in step 2. While custard is chilling, sprinkle sliced berries with remaining 3 tablespoons sugar and vanilla extract. Crush fruit lightly with potato masher (*see* figure 23) and refrigerate at least 1 hour to macerate. Add fruit mixture to ice cream about 1 minute before churning is completed.

Figure 23.
Place the sliced strawberries in a wide, shallow bowl. Sprinkle
them with sugar and vanilla and use a potato masher to lightly
crush the fruit. Allow the fruit to stand for about 1 hour or until
softened into a chunky puree.

Raspberry Ice Cream

➤ **N O T E :** *Unlike strawberries, raspberries do not really add any bulk to ice cream. The macerated berries are pushed through a fine-mesh strainer to remove the seeds, and the berry liquid is then stirred into a basic custard for a brightly colored and flavored ice cream.*

1½	**cups whole milk**
1½	**cups heavy cream**
⅞	**cup sugar**
4	**large egg yolks**
2	**cups raspberries**
1	**teaspoon vanilla extract**

I N S T R U C T I O N S :

Follow Master Recipe instructions for Vanilla Ice Cream (*see* page 30). While custard is chilling, sprinkle berries with remaining 2 tablespoons sugar and vanilla extract. Crush fruit lightly with potato masher (*see* figure 23, page 61) and refrigerate at least 1 hour to macerate. When fruit has softened, pour into fine-mesh strainer and press on solids to extract as much liquid as possible (*see* figure 24). Discard seeds and stir strained puree into chilled custard. Churn as directed.

V A R I A T I O N :

For Blackberry Ice Cream, replace raspberries with 2 cups blackberries.

Figure 24.
Raspberries and blackberries should be macerated like strawberries. However, the seeds in these smaller berries should be
strained out. Pour the softened berries into a fine-mesh strainer
and use the back of a large spoon or spatula to push the puree
through the strainer. Discard the seeds and use the strained liquid
to flavor the custard.

63

Peach Ice Cream

➤ **NOTE:** *Depending on how firm the peaches are, see figure 25 or 26 for tips on removing the skins. Firm peaches may be used in this recipe, but they should be sweet and flavorful. Peach-flavored liqueur or brandy intensifies the fruit flavor in this lightly perfumed ice cream.*

1	**cup whole milk**
1	**cup heavy cream**
¾	**cup sugar**
3	**large egg yolks**
3	**medium peaches (about 1 pound), peeled, pitted (*see* figures 25–8), and cut into ½-inch dice**
2	**tablespoons peach-flavored liqueur**
1	**teaspoon vanilla extract**

⁞ INSTRUCTIONS:

Follow Master Recipe instructions for Vanilla Ice Cream (*see* page 30), adding ¼ cup sugar to milk-cream mixture and beating another ¼ cup sugar with egg yolks. While custard is chilling, place peaches and their juices along with remaining ¼ cup sugar in large skillet. Cook over medium heat, stirring frequently, until juices thicken and caramelize, about 15 minutes. Stir in liqueur and cook another 2 minutes.

Remove pan from heat and chill peach mixture. Add vanilla to chilled custard and churn as directed. Add fruit mixture
to ice cream about 1 minute before churning is completed.

Figure 25.
*If the peaches are firm but ripe, you may use a vegetable peeler to
remove the skin from the fruit.*

Figure 26.
If the peaches are soft, drop them into a pot of boiling water for
10 seconds to loosen their skins. Retrieve the peaches with a slot-
ted spoon, cool slighlty, and then use a paring knife to scrape
away the skins.

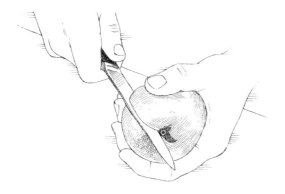

Figure 27.
To pit peaches, begin by running a small, sharp knife in a circle
around each peeled peach, making sure to cut through the stem end.

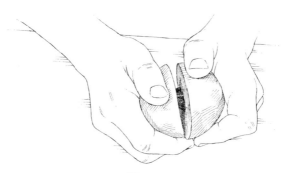

Figure 28.
Twist the peach halves to separate them. Remove the pit and
chop the peaches into ½-inch pieces.

67

Cherry Ice Cream

➤ **NOTE:** *Use a cherry pitter to prepare the cherries or* see *figures 29 and 30 if you prefer to remove the pits by hand.*

1½	cups whole milk
1½	cups heavy cream
1	cup sugar
4	large egg yolks
¾	pound ripe cherries, pitted
2	teaspoons vanilla extract

INSTRUCTIONS:

Follow Master Recipe instructions for Vanilla Ice Cream (*see* page 30). While custard is chilling, place cherries and remaining ¼ cup sugar in medium skillet. Cook over medium-high heat, crushing cherries with back of spoon until thick and syrupy, 10 to 15 minutes. Chill cherry mixture. Add vanilla to chilled custard and churn as directed. Add cherry mixture to ice cream about 1 minute before churning is completed.

VARIATION:

For Cherry Chocolate Chunk Ice Cream, add 2 ounces chopped bittersweet or semisweet chocolate bar (*see* figure 15, page 41) about 30 seconds before churning is completed.

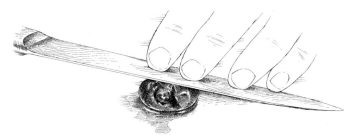

Figure 29.
*If you don't own a cherry pitter, try this technique for removing
the pits by hand. Use the side of a chef's knife to gently press
down on the side of the cherry and loosen the pit.*

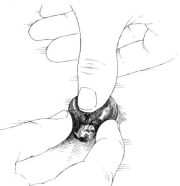

Figure 30.
*With your index finger and thumb on one hand and your thumb
on the second hand, gently squeeze the cherry slightly below the
bottom of the pit. The pit should come right out the top of the
cherry with a minimal loss of juices or pulp.*

69

Banana Ice Cream

➤ NOTE: *Straining the bananas (*see *figures 31 and 32) removes all the fibers and solids and gives this ice cream a smooth, silky texture. If desired, mash and strain two bananas and cut the third banana into ¼-inch cubes and add them to the ice cream about 30 seconds before churning is completed.*

1½	cups whole milk
1½	cups heavy cream
¾	cup sugar
4	large egg yolks
3	very ripe medium bananas, peeled, mashed with a fork, and strained (*see* figures 31 and 32)
2	teaspoons vanilla extract

∷ INSTRUCTIONS:

Follow Master Recipe instructions for Vanilla Ice Cream (*see* page 30), cooling custard until warm. Stir in strained bananas and chill to 40 degrees. Add vanilla extract and churn as directed.

∷ VARIATIONS:

For Banana Walnut Ice Cream, add 2 ounces chopped, toasted walnuts about 30 seconds before churning is completed. *See* figure 18, page 48, for information on toasting nuts.

70

For Banana Chocolate Chunk Ice Cream, add 2 ounces chopped bittersweet or semisweet chocolate bar about 30 seconds before churning is completed. *See* figure 15, page 41, for information on chopping a chocolate bar for ice cream.

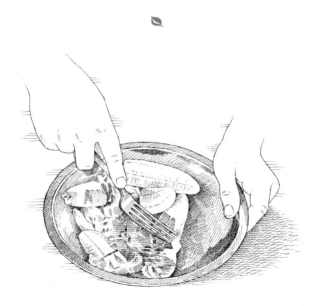

Figure 31.
Place the peeled ripe bananas in a medium bowl and mash them
with a fork until smooth.

Figure 32.

*Transfer the mashed bananas to a fine-mesh strainer and press
the bananas with a rubber spatula into a clean bowl. Discard the
fibers in the strainer and use the smooth banana puree to flavor
the custard.*

Rum Raisin Ice Cream

➤ **NOTE:** *Dark rum will add more flavor to this ice cream and is recommended. The alcohol will prevent this ice cream from firming up completely as it churns. Plan on placing the ice cream in the freezer for several hours before serving.*

½   **cup dark rum**

¾   **cup raisins**

1½   **cups whole milk**

1½   **cups heavy cream**

¾   **cup sugar**

4   **large egg yolks**

INSTRUCTIONS:

Follow Master Recipe instructions for Vanilla Ice Cream (*see* page 30), omitting vanilla from custard. Before making custard, warm rum and raisins in small saucepan. Remove pan from heat and steep 30 minutes. Drain and reserve rum and raisins separately. Stir rum into strained custard and chill. About 30 seconds before churning is completed, add reserved raisins.

chapter five

🝮

GELATO

ELATO IS ITALIAN ICE CREAM. ALTHOUGH the ingredients are similar to American ice cream, the results are surprisingly different. First of all, gelato is often made with flavors we rarely see in America. Hazelnut and the combination of hazelnuts and chocolate, called gianduja, are as common in Italian ice cream shops as vanilla or strawberry.

Of course, Italians make coffee gelato, but since coffee ice cream is a common American flavor we have not included this recipe. In addition to hazelnut and gianduja, you will find recipes for fig, amaretti, and cinnamon gelato in this chapter.

Besides unusual flavors, many American visitors to Italy

are struck by the intensity of the flavors in gelato. Gelato should not contain a hint of hazelnuts or cinnamon, rather a strong jolt. Many gelato recipes use large amounts of flavoring ingredients, and some add liqueurs for a further boost. While American ice cream is often about the cream, gelato is about the flavorings.

There are several reasons for this difference. In general, American ice cream contains more butterfat. The additional fat coats our tongues and dulls the perception of flavors. While we find that American ice cream is best made with equal parts heavy cream and whole milk, gelato requires a lighter hand, with almost two parts milk for each part cream. The texture will be less indulgent and rich, but the flavors are more intense.

Another important difference is temperature. Gelaterias in Italy generally serve their product at a higher temperature than do American ice cream shops. Because cold dulls flavors, a higher serving temperature heightens the intensity of gelato. It also makes gelato less icy and helps counteract the lower butterfat content.

We find that gelato tastes best when served at 15 degrees, about five degrees higher than American ice cream. At this temperature, gelato will not be as firm as ice cream, and it should be eaten with a spoon (as it is in Italy) and not licked from a cone.

Hazelnut Gelato

➤ **NOTE:** *Toasting the hazelnuts twice, once before skinning and once after, gives you an incredibly delicious and intense nut flavor.*

2	cups shelled hazelnuts, toasted, skinned, and toasted again (*see* figures 33–36)
2¼	cups whole milk
1¼	cups heavy cream
¾	cup sugar
4	large egg yolks
1	tablespoon Frangelico or other hazelnut liqueur (optional)
½	teaspoon vanilla extract

INSTRUCTIONS:

Follow Master Recipe instructions for Vanilla Ice Cream (*see* page 30). Before making custard, grind nuts in food processor and then add them to almost-simmering milk and cream. Remove pan from heat and steep 30 minutes. Pour through fine-mesh strainer and into clean saucepan, pressing down on nuts to extract as much liquid as possible. Discard nuts. Add ½ cup sugar to saucepan and heat mixture to 175 degrees. Proceed with recipe as directed, stirring in optional Frangelico with vanilla.

Figure 33.
Toasting hazelnuts loosens their bitter skins and brings out their
flavor. Start by toasting the nuts in a 350-degree oven until they
are fragrant and their skins are starting to blister and crack, about
15 minutes. Transfer the nuts to the center of a clean tea towel.

Figure 34.
Bring up the sides of the tea towel and twist it closed to seal in the nuts.

Figure 35.
Rub the nuts together through the towel to scrape off as much of
the brown skin as possible. It's fine if patches of skin remain.

Figure 36.
Carefully open the towel on a flat work surface. Gently roll the
nuts away from the skins. Return the nuts to the oven and toast
them until they have a rich golden color, about 15 minutes.

Gianduja Gelato

➤ **NOTE:** *The combination of chocolate and hazelnuts, called giunduja, is a classic in Italian cakes, candies, and ice creams.*

2	cups shelled hazelnuts, toasted, skinned, and toasted again (*see* figures 33–36, page 77)
2¼	cups whole milk
1¼	cups heavy cream
¾	cup sugar
4	large egg yolks
¼	cup unsweetened cocoa powder, preferably Dutch-process
1	tablespoon hazelnut liqueur (optional)
½	teaspoon vanilla extract

INSTRUCTIONS:

Follow Master Recipe instructions for Vanilla Ice Cream (*see* page 30). Before making custard, grind nuts in food processor and then add to almost-simmering milk and cream. Remove pan from heat and steep 30 minutes. Pour through fine-mesh strainer and into clean saucepan, pressing down on nuts to extract as much liquid as possible. Discard nuts. Add ½ cup sugar to saucepan and heat mixture to 175 degrees. Proceed with recipe as directed, adding cocoa to egg yolk–sugar mixture (*see* figure 17, page 43). Stir in optional liqueur with vanilla.

80

Fig Gelato

➤ **NOTE:** *In season, many Italian gelaterias use fresh figs. Dried figs are more reliable and give gelato an even more intense flavor. Light brown calimyrna figs work especially well in this recipe.*

1	cup dried figs (about ¼ pound), minced
2	cups whole milk
1	cup heavy cream
¾	cup sugar
4	large egg yolks
1	teaspoon vanilla extract

▪▪ INSTRUCTIONS:

Follow Master Recipe instructions for Vanilla Ice Cream (*see* page 30). Before making custard, place figs and ¾ cup water in 2½-quart saucepan. Simmer until figs are tender and liquid is nearly evaporated, about 10 minutes. Stir in ½ cup sugar and cook, stirring often, until dissolved. Add milk and cream and heat to 175 degrees. Proceed with recipe, beating remaining sugar and egg yolks as directed.

Amaretti Gelato

➤ **NOTE:** *Crisp almond macaroons, known in Italian as amaretti, are sold in better supermarkets and Italian foods shops. Since the cookies are crumbled, either large or small amaretti will work in this recipe. See figure 16, page 41, for information on crumbling cookies for ice cream.*

2	cups whole milk
1	cup heavy cream
¾	cup sugar
4	large egg yolks
3	tablespoons Amaretto or almond-flavored liqueur
1	cup crumbled amaretti cookies

INSTRUCTIONS:

Follow Master Recipe instructions for Vanilla Ice Cream (*see* page 30), replacing vanilla with Amaretto. About 30 seconds before churning is completed, add crumbled amaretti cookies.

Cinnamon Gelato

➤ NOTE: *Ground cinnamon gives this gelato a warm, rich flavor that is distinctively Italian. Make sure your cinnamon is fresh.*

2 **cups whole milk**
1 **cup heavy cream**
2 **teaspoons ground cinnamon**
¾ **cup sugar**
4 **large egg yolks**
1 **teaspoon vanilla extract**

∷ INSTRUCTIONS:

Follow Master Recipe instructions for Vanilla Ice Cream (*see* page 30), stirring cinnamon into ½ cup sugar (*see* figure 21, page 55) and then adding mixture to milk and cream in step 1.

chapter six

SAUCES AND
ACCOMPANIMENTS

I CE CREAM CAN BE ENJOYED ON ITS OWN OR SERVED
à la mode with a slice of pie. However, there are
times when a spoonful of hot fudge sauce and a
dollop of whipped cream are appropriate. This
chapter contains a variety of classic American sauces for ice
cream along with our foolproof technique for whipping
cream.

The sauce recipes that follow may be used on their own
with ice cream or as part of sundaes. One-quarter cup of
sauce makes a generous topping for two scoops of ice
cream. Most sauces may be prepared well in advance and
stored in the refrigerator for days, if not weeks. Sauces that

are best eaten warm, such as hot fudge, should be heated in a double boiler or microwave as needed.

Sundaes are as all-American as apple pie, maybe even more so because they were actually invented in this country just before the turn of the century. The precise origins of the ice cream sundae are a bit murky. Several sources cite nineteenth-century prohibitions against the drinking of soda water on the Sabbath. With popular ice cream sodas out of bounds, ice cream parlors started serving sauces and other toppings with ice cream on Sunday.

However the practice began, a sundae appeals to children as well as adults. Spoon one-quarter cup of any of the following sauce recipes over two scoops of ice cream and then top off with a one-half-cup or generous three-quarter-cup dollop of whipped cream. A sprinkling of chopped, toasted walnuts and a maraschino cherry finish off a classic sundae.

Hot Fudge Sauce

➤ **NOTE:** *This recipe produces a thick, chewy sauce that hardens when poured over cold ice cream. We love hot fudge sauce over most any ice cream. This recipe makes about two and one-quarter cups.*

10	ounces semisweet chocolate, chopped
3	tablespoons unsalted butter, cut into pieces
¼	cup sifted Dutch-process cocoa powder
¾	cup sugar
¾	cup heavy cream
3	tablespoons light corn syrup
	Pinch salt
1	teaspoon vanilla extract

INSTRUCTIONS:

1. Melt chocolate and butter together, stirring often, in small heatproof bowl set over pan of almost-simmering water. Off heat, whisk in cocoa powder until lumps dissolve. Set aside.

2. Combine sugar, cream, corn syrup, salt, and 2 tablespoons water in heavy-bottomed nonreactive saucepan. Cook over medium-low heat, stirring constantly and scraping pot sides occasionally until mixture comes to boil. Simmer, stirring constantly to keep sauce from boiling over (*see* figure 37), until all sugar dissolves, about 2 minutes.

86

3. Remove pan from heat. Stir in vanilla and cool 2 minutes. Whisk in melted chocolate and butter. Mixture will thicken slightly as it cools. Serve sauce warm. Sauce may be refrigerated in airtight container for several weeks. Reheat sauce gently in double boiler.

Figure 37.

When the sugar, cream, corn syrup, and water mixture comes to a boil it will quickly increase in volume. To keep the foaming mixture from rising out of the pan, stir constantly with a wooden spoon. This mixture must be cooked until all the sugar dissolves, about 2 minutes.

Classic Caramel Sauce

➤ **N O T E :** *This smooth, silky sauce is a great match with maple walnut, butter pecan, vanilla, or any banana ice cream. This recipe makes about one and three-quarters cups.*

1½	cups sugar
1	cup heavy cream

▉ I N S T R U C T I O N S :

1. Place sugar and ½ cup water in medium, heavy-bottomed saucepan. Turn heat to medium-low and stir often until sugar dissolves. Increase heat to high and cook, without stirring but swirling pan occasionally (*see* figure 38), until caramel is uniformly golden amber color, 8 to 10 minutes.

2. Put on oven mitts to protect hands. Remove pan from heat and slowly whisk in cream a few tablespoons at a time, making sure to keep bubbling caramel away from arms. Stir until smooth. Sauce thickens as it cools. Serve warm or at room temperature. Sauce may be refrigerated in airtight container for several weeks. Reheat sauce in microwave or double boiler before using.

Figure 38.
When making caramel sauce, do not stir once the sugar has dis-
solved. However, do swirl the sauce occasionally by holding the
handle and moving the pan back and forth across the burner.

Best Butterscotch Sauce

➤ **NOTE:** *Light brown sugar gives this sauce a more intense caramelized flavor than that of plain caramel sauce. The butter gives it a richer mouth feel as well. This recipe yields about one and one-half cups.*

1	cup firmly packed light brown sugar
¼	cup light corn syrup
3	tablespoons unsalted butter
	Pinch salt
½	cup heavy cream
1½	teaspoons vanilla extract

INSTRUCTIONS:

1. Combine sugar, corn syrup, butter, and salt in small, heavy-bottomed saucepan. Cook over medium heat, stirring often, until sugar melts.

2. Reduce heat to low and simmer without stirring until syrup reaches 280 degrees on candy thermometer, about 10 minutes.

3. Remove pan from heat and slowly stir in cream until sauce is smooth. Stir in vanilla. Sauce thickens as it cools. Serve warm or at room temperature. Sauce may be refrigerated in airtight container for several weeks. Reheat sauce in microwave or double boiler before using.

Melba Sauce

➢ NOTE: *Melba sauce is a fancy name for raspberry sauce. It's wonderful over vanilla ice cream with sliced fruit, especially peaches. If you like, stir in one-half cup lightly crushed fresh raspberries just before serving. Without the fresh berries, this recipe yields about one cup.*

1	12-ounce package frozen raspberries, thawed
½	cup sugar
1	tablespoon lemon juice

∷ INSTRUCTIONS:

1. Place berries and sugar in small saucepan. Cook, stirring often, over medium heat until sugar dissolves and berries soften, 3 to 4 minutes.

2. Remove pan from heat and stir in lemon juice. Transfer sauce to fine-mesh strainer set over small bowl. Press on solids to extract as much liquid as possible. Discard seeds. Serve at room temperature. Sauce may be refrigerated in airtight container for several days.

Warm Bing Cherry Sauce

➤ NOTE: *This sauce is wonderful over vanilla ice cream. Use fresh fruit as directed below or a twelve-ounce bag of frozen pitted cherries, which will work just fine. Fresh cherries may be pitted by hand (see figures 29 and 30, page 69) or with a cherry pitter. This recipe yields about one and one-half cups.*

1	pound cherries, pitted
½	cup sugar
¼	cup light corn syrup
¼	cup brandy
2	teaspoons cornstarch
½	teaspoon lemon juice
⅛	teaspoon almond extract

▪▪ INSTRUCTIONS:

1. Place cherries, sugar, corn syrup, and brandy in medium saucepan. Bring to boil, lower heat, and simmer, stirring occasionally and using back of spoon to gently break apart cherries, until sauce thickens slightly, about 8 minutes.

2. Remove pan from heat. Stir cornstarch and 1 tablespoon cold water together in small bowl. Add cornstarch mixture to sauce and stir until incorporated.

3. Return pan to heat and bring sauce to boil. Simmer, stirring constantly, until sauce thickens, about 1 minute.

4. Remove pan from heat and stir in lemon juice and almond extract. Sauce thickens as it cools. Serve warm. Sauce may be refrigerated in airtight container for several days. Reheat sauce in microwave or double boiler before using.

Perfect Whipped Cream

➤ **NOTE:** *Pasteurized cream has a superior flavor to ultrapasteurized cream and delivers more volume when whipped. Use either, but note that pasteurized cream overwhips more quickly, so you may prefer to slightly underwhip it, then remove the beaters and handwhip the cream a few strokes to the desired consistency. This recipe makes about four cups, a generous amount for six sundaes.*

> 2 **cups chilled heavy cream**
> 2 **tablespoons granulated sugar**
> 2 **teaspoons vanilla extract**

⁝⁝ INSTRUCTIONS:

1. Chill nonreactive, deep 2-quart bowl and beaters for handheld mixer in freezer at least 20 minutes.

2. Add cream, sugar, and vanilla to chilled bowl. Beat on low speed until small bubbles form, about 30 seconds. Increase speed to medium; continue beating until beaters leave a trail in thickening cream, about 30 seconds. Increase speed to high; continue beating until cream is smooth, thick, and nearly doubled in volume, about 30 seconds for soft peaks (*see* figure 39) and about 40 seconds for stiff peaks (*see* figure 40). If necessary, finish beating by hand to adjust consistency.

3. Use immediately or transfer to fine sieve or strainer set over bowl and refrigerate for up to 8 hours.

3. Return pan to heat and bring sauce to boil. Simmer, stirring constantly, until sauce thickens, about 1 minute.

4. Remove pan from heat and stir in lemon juice and almond extract. Sauce thickens as it cools. Serve warm. Sauce may be refrigerated in airtight container for several days. Reheat sauce in microwave or double boiler before using.

Perfect Whipped Cream

➤ **N O T E :** *Pasteurized cream has a superior flavor to ultrapasteurized cream and delivers more volume when whipped. Use either, but note that pasteurized cream overwhips more quickly, so you may prefer to slightly underwhip it, then remove the beaters and handwhip the cream a few strokes to the desired consistency. This recipe makes about four cups, a generous amount for six sundaes.*

> 2 **cups chilled heavy cream**
> 2 **tablespoons granulated sugar**
> 2 **teaspoons vanilla extract**

I N S T R U C T I O N S :

1. Chill nonreactive, deep 2-quart bowl and beaters for handheld mixer in freezer at least 20 minutes.

2. Add cream, sugar, and vanilla to chilled bowl. Beat on low speed until small bubbles form, about 30 seconds. Increase speed to medium; continue beating until beaters leave a trail in thickening cream, about 30 seconds. Increase speed to high; continue beating until cream is smooth, thick, and nearly doubled in volume, about 30 seconds for soft peaks (*see* figure 39) and about 40 seconds for stiff peaks (*see* figure 40). If necessary, finish beating by hand to adjust consistency.

3. Use immediately or transfer to fine sieve or strainer set over bowl and refrigerate for up to 8 hours.

Figure 39.
Cream whipped to soft peaks
will droop slightly from the
ends of the beaters.

Figure 40.
Cream whipped to stiff
peaks will cling tightly to
the ends of the beaters.
Cream is traditionally
whipped to this stage for
ice cream sundaes.

95

i n d e x